The UNIVERSAL MANAGEMENT PRINCIPLE

Workbook

How to Motivate Your Team Better

Richard Huttner

Successful Manager Enterprises, Gloucester, MA

Successful Manager Enterprises, Registered Offices, 29B Kennedy Road, Gloucester, MA 01930

Book design by Melvyn Paulino

Printed in the United States of America

ISBN-978-1-7323078-0-3

Empathy is one of the greatest creators of energy."

— *Angela Ahrendts,*
Senior Vice President of Retail at Apple,
on how she motivates her team.

Acknowledgments

My wife, Marcia Huttner, was an inspiration to me during the writing of this book and never wavered in her confidence that it contained an important, valuable message. My son, Matthew, provided excellent feedback on the draft manuscript, enabling me to write a much improved and appropriate final version. Thanks go also to my daughter, Elizabeth Huttner-Loan, and to my sister, Hilary Fylstra, for their comments, enthusiasm, and support. I also want to express my appreciation to Dan Fylstra for his supplying one of the book's key stories.

Lastly, I thank Howard Morhaim and Denise Marcil for their advice and help and Kim-Mei Kirtland for her editorial assistance.

TABLE OF CONTENTS

Introduction

Throughout my 40+ year career as a senior executive and entrepreneur, I have enjoyed a variety of management chal-lenges. I served as a division head at large companies like American Express and Time Warner and as the CEO at smaller companies like Parenting Unlimited, Senior Golfer, and Weider Health and Fitness (UK).

I've also had a second career in leadership and management skills training as the COO of the prestigious Levinson Institute in Boston and as the owner of the Massachusetts franchise of Crestcom International, a worldwide leadership skills training company. Over 50 MA companies placed their trust in me by sending their middle and senior executives to my year-long seminar series.

For several years, I taught entrepreneurship and organizational behavior at Northeastern's University's D'Amore-McKim School of Business. I am a *cum laude* graduate of Yale and have an MBA from the Stanford Graduate School of Business.

Out of all this experience, two thoughts relevant to this book's introduction come to mind: one, I can't remember anyone on my management team ever voluntarily leaving my company; two, I've produced excellent results using the techniques in this book: one of the businesses I've led achieved a 24% annualized sales growth rate and another, a 35% compounded return on equity.

My success relates to what I call "The Universal Management Principle."

"People don't care how much you know until they know how much you care."

This book is about this truth and how you, as a manager, can use eight fundamental techniques stemming from it to motivate your team better. The methods work equally well in business, in academia, or in government. Research studies over the last fifty years document their effectiveness. My goal is to help you to understand these techniques better and to use them to your benefit.

The aphorism, "People don't care how much you know until they know how much you care," is generally attributed to President Theodore Roosevelt although we don't know when and where he actually said it. Whatever its origin, this insightful saying gets right to the heart of human motivation.

Try to visualize the Universal Management Principle as the hub of a motivational wheel. This book's chapters are the spokes. You can seize upon any of them to give your team a vital motivational push. Which ones you choose depends upon your comfort level, your

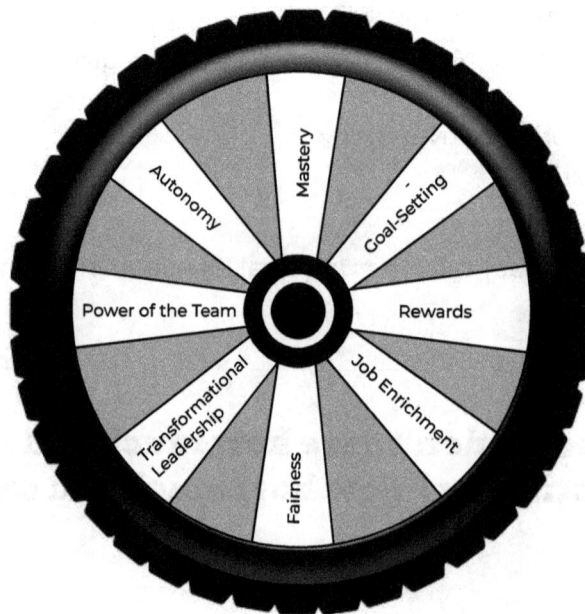

individual team member needs, and the situation. By keeping the Universal Management Principle in mind, you'll always be able to choose the right technique or the most effective combination.

To speed your learning, this workbook cites relevant research and includes many illustrative examples. As you finish each chapter, I encourage you to stop, think through each technique, and document how best to apply it. You can do this easily by answering the end-of-chapter challenge questions.

For your further convenience, I have included a summary chart at the end of the book for you to list your action steps. The chart has a column for each technique and a row for each of your team members. You can, of course, use any format you like; what is important is for you *to commit yourself to implementing what you have learned.*

These techniques work. Clear evidence comes from Google's 2009 "Project Oxygen" in-depth study of what makes a good manager. Since Google is one of the world's foremost technology companies, researchers expected its highest-ranked managers would be those with deep technical expertise.

In actuality, "What employees valued most were even-keeled bosses who made time for one-on-one meetings, who helped people puzzle through problems by asking questions, not dictating answers, and who took an interest in employees' lives and careers."

If you are the head of a business, I cite evidence that the techniques in this book could result in an increase of 20 percent or higher in your company's growth and profitability. If you are managing a work group at any level, you'll see your team members grow in enthusiasm, confidence, and productivity. Lastly, you will experience the satisfaction of becoming a much more effective leader yourself.

Chapter 1

Autonomy

Empowering team members with sufficient autonomy is an essential motivating principle. *People like to do what they want to do, when they want to do it.* A manager who takes away autonomy takes away motivation. Here is a typical example of how a manager with the best of intentions can fall into this trap.

Caroline Traynor (all case names and companies in the book are fictional) is a Boston-based account executive at Marketing Synergistics. Her company builds customized marketing models that help clients track customer responses across multiple marketing channels. These models answer questions like: "Did a customer inquiry originate from an Internet search, a website ad, a social media response, or an email campaign? How do different marketing programs interact to drive sales?" Caroline likes to say that Marketing Synergistics helps marketers see the sales forest through the Internet trees.

Her account executive role is especially challenging because the company's model builders are located in Mumbai, India, and this can cause communication problems. In Indian business culture, it is considered impolite to give a direct negative response. When she voices a project-specific concern, her Indian counterparts may say, "This does not sound like a significant problem," "Yes, you think the model should have this?" or "That's

an excellent idea." The Indian team's unstated expectation is that everything will somehow work out alright. Her understanding is that the model will *definitely* contain the specified features. Because of this communications disconnect, customers are sometimes disappointed with how their models work.

To make sure her technical team delivers precisely what her customers want, Caroline has created a highly effective system that allows her to track deadlines carefully and double-check model features. Now she knows that the models will work as expected. She is also proud of having met the communications challenge of operating in a multicultural environment.

One day, her sales team head, Tom Montgomery, gives her a new assignment. "Caroline," he says excitedly, "I've talked with our senior people here and in Mumbai. Since you have been so successful in communicating with the Indian team, I want you to take your system company-wide.

"Please document all your current methods so we can make them official policy. Then, come up with new ways we can guarantee on-time, accurate model delivery. Each month, give me at least three good ideas for how the US and Indian staffs can work better together. I am sure this will make a huge difference in company morale and customer satisfaction."

At first, Caroline is flattered that Tom is entrusting her with such an important responsibility. By the third month of submitting ideas, however, she finds she is running out of them. The new responsibility is quickly becoming a dreaded chore.

What has happened? Why is this challenge, which Caroline's manager thought would be so motivating, turning out to be *demotivating*? The answer is that, before, Caroline had the freedom to be creative. Now that she is being *forced* to do what she previously did voluntarily, she doesn't like her job as much. Her manager's assignment has intruded upon her autonomy. *People like to do what they want to do, when they want to do it.*

This fundamental human drive for autonomy starts early in life. Anyone who has ever watched a toddler play has observed it. One minute, she is playing with a stuffed animal; the next, trying to open a playpen gate, pouring imaginary tea from a play tea set, mailing a letter in a child-sized wood mailbox, or stacking brightly colored plastic rings. Caregivers who interfere with this freedom to play do so at their peril. If they are not skilled at distracting the child with an activity she wants to do even more, caregivers get immediate resistance. No wonder parents are often mentally and physically exhausted at the end of the day while the toddler is (hopefully) peacefully asleep, having done what toddlers are born to do.

For most of us, this need for autonomy carries forward throughout life and finds its natural expression in the workplace.

> ## "
> ### People Want Power Because They Want Autonomy"
>
> – *The Atlantic Daily*,
> March 22, 2016

Autonomy is especially important in jobs that require independent thought, creativity, and long-term emotional commitment. In such knowledge work, team members are most enthusiastic when they can *carve out for themselves* the best way to succeed.

Today, the majority of jobs require this freedom. A good manager lets team members decide how to execute their responsibilities, when to take the initiative, whom to consult or contact, and which procedures to use. Assuming you, as a manager, have placed the right people in the right roles, you'll see team members performing at their best *when they are truly in charge.*

On the other hand, as Caroline's example shows, when a manager effectively forces an employee to do something – even something the employee previously liked – resistance sets in. John Hersey, the motivational speaker and author of *Creating Contagious Leadership*, once remarked, "You can't make employees really *do anything*." In the long run, I think he is right.

To make sure you avoid micromanaging, ask yourself, "Do I really trust my team members? Am I doing more *asking* than *telling*? Do I show sufficient confidence in my team members' abilities that I let them solve problems in their own way?"

The following story illustrates how important it is to be able to answer "Yes" to these questions.

Charlene Kensey is the General Manager of Electro Cable, a Midwestern company that manufactures cable assemblies, test boxes, and control panels for customers in the medical instrumentation and aerospace industries.

One of her key team members, Bill Wu, is a valued employee. He started at the company 20 years ago on the cable manufacturing assembly line. Today, he heads Electro Cable's Request for Proposal (RFP) Department. Every day, Bill receives bid invitations from companies all over the world. Bill and his staff review each one, establish pricing, and promptly submit completed bids.

Charlene believes that instead of just responding to RFPs, Bill should reach out more and try to forge partnerships with these large prospective customers. Fired up, Charlene calls Bill into her office. "Bill, from now on, for all significant bid requests, I'd like you to pick up the phone and see first if you can get us a meeting. Let's get out there and see these project managers with whom we normally only communicate by phone or email. My goal is to build proprietary relationships that generate new sales. I want you to become our ambassador."

Bill sits in shocked silence. He is a reserved, inner-directed person most comfortable with numbers. He suffers from mild social anxiety. He does not view "getting out there" as something he wants to do.

A month goes by, and there is no buzz about new prospective customer meetings. When Charlene talks with Bill, he always smiles, says he is working on setting them up, and, as if to change the topic, mentions some exciting new bids in the works.

Charlene keeps pushing. "Bill, I need you to be more aggressive in reaching out.

I'm sure many of these companies are open to engaging with us. You're not letting them know about our new full-service approach."

Do you think Bill ever steps out of his comfort zone, initiating blue-sky discussions with bid requesters about how the two companies might work together? No way. He simply *continues to do the parts of his job that he likes*. His resistance is unassailable. As he is such a long-term, well-regarded, and valuable employee, Charlene has no alternative but to call upon less qualified, but more outgoing, team members to take the sales lead.

If Charlene had *asked* Bill how he and his team might reach out to customers better, who knows what good ideas he might have come up with? Bill might have deputized some of his extroverted staff members to make the calls under his direction, thereby preserving his autonomy.

The moral of the story is be wary of telling team members exactly what to do.

Preserving autonomy, however, does not mean that a manager should give team members complete freedom. At certain times, such as for regulatory or safety reasons, or during a crisis, a company or a manager must require employees to adhere to specific policies and practices, whether they like them or not.

When there's a good reason for such directives, employees don't object. If a particular kind of work necessitates team members wearing a uniform, using standard software, or treating customers in a certain way, almost all will accept willingly these rules and practices.

> ❝
>
> **Never tell people how to do things. Tell them what to do and they will surprise you with their ingenuity.**"
>
> –General George S. Patton

Let's now look at autonomy enhancers for greater motivation. A major one, research shows, is to assure team members are fully-prepared to take on their assignments. You cannot ask a team member to do something for which they lack the skills. Not being prepared generates anxiety that interferes with motivation and performance. Letting a team member "figure it out" can be overwhelming.

I heard many examples of this when I taught organizational behavior at Northeastern University. All my students had worked at three-month "co-ops" as part of Northeastern's five-year college curriculum. They had interned at a wide variety of companies, from industrial, consumer, and financial firms to digital start-ups and consulting boutiques.

A significant number told similar stories of being introduced on day one to their managers, meeting everyone in the office, and looking forward to a rewarding work experience only to become, within weeks, profoundly disappointed.

A primary reason was frustration. Their co-workers or supervisors may have been familiar with the company's systems and operations, how projects flowed from one department to another, or whom to go to when problems arose, but these students weren't. They were so at sea that they sometimes felt helpless and eventually became so unhappy that they simply checked out at work.

These "newbie" problems may have been extreme; nevertheless, they illustrate that team members need to feel competent and confident.

Another important autonomy amplifier is that they need to feel connected to their leader and to other team members. Most want their managers to be aware of their progress and interested in their achievements. They want to share their results with their peers, too.

"

Control leads to compliance; autonomy leads to engagement."

–Daniel H. Pink, author of *Drive*

Such social interaction has the additional benefit of providing opportunity for valued feedback. This helps team members correct course when necessary. More mature team members especially appreciate this input.

To sum up, if you want to be a successful motivator, keep autonomy for your team members at the top of your list: Guide rather than dictate; let your team members have the scope their positions need and merit. Then, build team members' competence and confidence by making sure they have the right skills and by offering your support and feedback. Remember to use The Universal Management Principle at every opportunity. *"People don't care how much you know until they know how much you care."*

If, after a reasonable time, however, a team member does not perform, despite your remedial efforts, then you must remove him from the team. Sometimes this is hard, of course, but such a change will almost always be for the good. It is better to take forceful action – even if your team or your company takes a short-term hit – than to let a bad situation fester and poison team morale. Hurtful or unethical behavior must be dealt with immediately. *No one should be immune or judged indispensable.*

Perhaps the illustration of a car, the "Autonomy-Mobile," will help you visualize the major lessons of this chapter. Autonomy is this car's motivational fuel and will speed the car forward. If you want the Autonomy-Mobile to really zoom along, keep in good shape the front tires of competence and confidence and the back tires of feedback and support.

Autonomy-Mobile

Feedback and Support   **Competence and Confidence**

Now, it is time for your first challenge questions which are on the worksheet on the next page. In thinking about your answers, keep in mind they will necessarily be different for each direct report. Some employees function very well on their own. The more experienced and confident a team member is, the more autonomy she may desire and be able to take on. Liberally granting it will free up your own time to focus on the long-range strategic issues vital to your team's success.

Autonomy Challenge Questions

1. How have you granted, or will grant, each team member sufficient autonomy to feel empowered and more motivated?

_____
_____
_____
_____
_____
_____
_____

2. What additional preparation is needed for each team member to feel fully competent and confident?

_____
_____
_____
_____
_____
_____
_____

3. How are you providing constructive feedback and needed support?

_____
_____
_____
_____
_____
_____

Chapter 2

Mastery

In our previous chapter, autonomy was the star; "competence and confidence" and "feedback and support" played supporting roles. Now is the time to bring these co-stars to center stage. They are foundational to the next motivational concept, *mastery*.

Mastery is the belief you have the skills, resources, and support to be successful. The concept goes beyond self-confidence because it includes not only having superior skills but also knowing you can call upon others when you need them.

Research confirms when we feel masterful we become more motivated because we expect future success and anticipate the self-satisfaction and pride it will bring. Think of this motivational cycle as having three steps: (1) expecting to be able to a good job, (2) having rewarding work experiences, and (3) looking forward to the next, higher achievement. I call this the Mastery Spiral.

The Mastery Spiral

Higher levels of mastery spawn higher levels of achievement

The obvious next question is: how do you build mastery in your team members? Start by giving them challenging assignments. These should not be so difficult as to be frustrating (as happened to my Northeastern students) nor so easy as to be boring. Get your team working "in the zone" where time seems to fly because one is so enjoyably and productively engaged. Did you ever hear one of your team members say enthusiastically, "I'd do that job even if I didn't get paid for it"? (Okay, I'm exaggerating.) The point is that successive challenging assignments build mastery because they boost team members' competence and confidence and instill a desire to do more.

Next, make time for important and necessary training. This raises the question of the proper kind. Here is an example of an all-too-common type of training that accomplishes relatively little.

Johnson Pump Co. is a wholesaler of pumps used to transport liquids. (My favorite application is beer brewing. If you've watched a craft beer-making display at a local pub, you've seen the brewing mix being pumped from tank to tank.) Johnson's competitive advantage is that it provides hands-on customer support. Its service staff fixes broken pumps in the field and has to be knowledgeable about the many types the company sells.

Tracy Johnson, a grand-daughter of the company's founder, is a new supervisor. She manages one of the field service teams. One morning, she attends a training session at one of Johnson Pump's suppliers. The training consists of a classroom session in which an instructor demonstrates how his company's pumps work and how, in some applications, they might freeze up. Tracy leaves the session with the pump manufacturer's latest catalog and some ancillary parts diagrams.

> ❝
> **You cannot have faith in people unless you take action to improve and develop them."**
>
> – Sumantra Ghoshal, Professor of Strategic and International Management at the London Business School

This type of "show and tell" training may give Tracy useful information, but it is unlikely that she will be confident enough, or even able, to fix a frozen pump in the field under a customer's watchful eye. The training is insufficient. She hasn't really mastered the task.

What type of training does elevate a team member's competence and self-confidence? The answer is "full commitment training." This type of training contains four steps. The first is for the trainee to attend a demonstration of the desired skill, as Tracy did. This is like a music student watching a master musician and thinking how much she would like to play that well.

The second step is practical, "how-to" training. If Tracy had attended a in-depth class in the afternoon, for example, she would have come away with a much more thorough understanding of how to repair pumps.

Just one hands-on class is still not enough to cement learning. The third step of full-commitment training is practice and coaching. Perhaps the manufacturer could invite Tracy to come in the next week to review and practice with an instructor what she had learned.

The fourth and last step of full-commitment training is real-world accomplishment. The first time Tracy, under pressure, successfully fixes a customer's frozen pump, her sense of mastery will soar. Moreover, she'll likely be thinking that she now has the ability to teach her team what she has learned.

To summarize, full commitment training entails:

1. A *demonstration* to provide basic information, dispel fears, and generate enthusiasm

2. *Hands-on learning* or role-playing

3. *Practicing* with a coach

4. *Real-world responsibility* and accomplishment

Full commitment training has additional benefits, such as employee retention. Most employees want to work for a manager who invests in them and seeks to grow their skills.[1] If a manager does this, the best team members are less likely to leave for greater opportunity. Furthermore, for some team members, full commitment training reduces stress, anxiety, and even depression. A sense of mastery can be an important healer.

The next point is few team members can continue to grow in mastery without their manager's on-going guidance.

Feedback and support are the teammates of competence and confidence. To remain optimistic and enthusiastic, team members want confirmation they are on the right track and a chance to improve if they are not.

> 66
> An empowered organization is one in which individuals have the knowledge, skill, desire, and opportunity to personally succeed in a way that leads to collective organizational success."
>
> – Stephen Covey, American educator

> 66
> Leadership is about making others better as a result of your presence and making sure that impact lasts in your absence."
>
> – Sheryl Sandberg, COO, Facebook

---

1 For example, David A. Garvin, Alison Berkley Wagonfeld, and Liz Kind, "Google's Project Oxygen: Do Managers Matter?" Harvard Business School Case 313-110, April 2013. (Revised October 2013.).

If a manager displays such excellent leadership skills, team members will respond by producing the desired results. How many times have you heard a story about an employee who, under the guidance of an involved manager and mentor, became a leader in the company?

This brings us to applying this chapter's information. Here are your challenge questions about using mastery as a motivator.

Mastery Challenge Questions

1. Do you have a plan for each of your team members to help them improve their skills and self-confidence? If not, can you create one?

_____

_____

_____

_____

_____

_____

2. Do you provide your team members "full commitment training?" What more should you be doing?

_____

_____

_____

_____

_____

_____

3. Are you being a mentor to your team members? Are you "growing" them through spending sufficient time with them and sharing your knowledge and wisdom?

_____

_____

_____

_____

_____

_____

Chapter 3

Goal-Setting

In the previous chapter, I talked about how giving team members challenging assignments builds mastery and increases motivation. What makes assignments challenging are clear, meaningful goals. The originators of goal-setting theory, professors Edwin A. Locke and Gary P. Latham, explain why goals are such effective motivators:

> Goals enhance performance because such goals clearly define acceptable levels of performance, increase the amount of effort an individual exerts, increase task persistence, lead to more extensive strategy development and planning, and orient individuals towards goal-related knowledge and activities.[2]

In other words, goals capture team members' imaginations, engage them, and focus their energies.

Second, *specific* goals like hitting a growth target work better than *general* goals like "Do your best." Specific goals inform team members of exactly what you want them to accomplish.

Third, as I intimated in the previous chapter, goals that are easy are boring, especially to team members who pride themselves on their abilities and achievements. Goals that are impossibly high are frustrating. Team members feel, "Why try?" "Stretch goals," on the other hand, to borrow from the Goldilocks story, are "just right." Stretch goals lead to maximum work satisfaction and high productivity. As renowned educator and motivational speaker Carl Boyd has famously said, "No one rises to low expectations."

If you are concerned that a stretch goal is overwhelming, you may want to break it down into a series of interim goals to make the final objective easier for your team member to reach. This approach works especially well with team members who feel uncomfortable under pressure or who get easily rattled. Interim goals also help procrastinators.

Fourth, team members will be more enthusiastic about reaching goals when they have participated in setting them. There is a saying: "Those who plan the battle rarely battle the plan." A robust discussion may also surface potential pitfalls, unearth creative approaches, and ultimately, save time and money.

Fifth, give your team members ongoing, but carefully chosen, feedback as they pursue their goals. I've mentioned this before: Encourage them to be open to course correction. Timely feedback demonstrates your willingness to help with problems and your interest in your team members' progress.

---

2 Neil Anderson et al., *Handbook of Industrial, Work & Organizational Psychology* (London: SAGE Publications, 2001) 2: 62.

Here is a step-by-step method you can use to set goal assignments in a way that will motivate your team members:

1. Explain the reasoning behind the assignment

When you were a kid, didn't you always want to know the reason why you had to do something? It's the same with adults. When team members know why they are being asked to do something, they are more enthusiastic about doing it. So, set context by explaining the assignment background and your current reasoning. This is also a mark of respect as team members will appreciate you are, in effect, taking them into your confidence.

2. Solicit team member input

Encourage your direct reports to then ask questions, express concerns, and offer suggestions. *There really may be a better way.* This dialogue, this sharing of information early on, will result in you and your team members setting more effective goals.

3. Define the QQTR

QQTR is a way of elegantly framing an assignment and letting the team member know exactly what has to be done. The acronym, originated by the Canadian management theorist Elliott Jaques, stands for:

Quantity of Work
Quality of Work
Time Frame for Completion
Resources available

> 66
>
> **Setting goals is the first step in turning the invisible into the visible."**
>
> – Tony Robins, author of *Awaken the Giant Within*

Here is an example of how a manager might use QQTR:

> *Barbara, I'd like you to analyze the last three years' sales for our top ten customers. I'd like to see a basic spreadsheet first, and then, after we have looked at it together, for you to create a series of charts designed to show the sales growth we've experienced with these leading customers.*
> **(Quantity of Work)**

> *Once you have the charts, please put them into an attractive PowerPoint presentation that I can show to our senior management team. The charts should have some bells and whistles that carry a strong visual message of sales growth. Please also prepare a condensed PDF version that I can email as to managers at other offices.*
> **(Quality of Work)**.

21

> *Let's plan for our first meeting next Wednesday. We can look at your data and see the trends. I'll need the full package of the PowerPoint presentation and the accompanying PDF by the following Friday. I have to meet with the senior team on Monday, so I'll have the weekend to look everything over.*
> **(Time Frame for Completion)**

> *Please make this your first priority. Ralph in accounting can supply the yearly sales numbers and assist you with the spreadsheet. Also, I suggest you work with Nancy; she's a wonderful PowerPoint designer. I'll give both these people a heads-up about being available to help you out."*
> **(Resources Available)**

Note that in the above example the manager never tells the team member exactly how to do the spreadsheet or charts. To be overly specific would take away Barbara's autonomy and undermine her sense of mastery. You want to give your team members the freedom to show their stuff.

4. Explain how you will use the team member's work

Have you ever experienced giving someone an assignment only to discover the work that they produce is not quite right or could have been done much better? You then have to ask for revisions, often on a tight deadline, or you have to do the extra work yourself. Project completion becomes quite stressful, and the team member may feel disappointed at not having nailed the assignment.

To be clear about what you truly want, discuss with your team member upfront *how the completed project might look if it fully met your expectations.*[3] In the above example, the manager might have told Barbara that he is debating whether or not to reallocate the company's resources to the top ten customers and that he needs a presentation so compelling that, if he decides to move in this direction, top management will be fully supportive.

> 66
>
> **One way to keep motivation going is to have constantly greater goals."**
>
> – Michael Korda,
> celebrated editor and writer

With this greater understanding of her manager's intentions, Barbara might include pertinent industry forecasts, interviews with key customers about the potential for additional business, and other useful information.

In short, the more your team member knows about what you intend to do with the assignment deliverable, the more complete and appropriate he or she can make it. As best-selling British business book author Andy Bounds points out, you'll get projects "done right the first time."[4]

5. Ask for questions

Normally, team members will have questions after you have given them an assignment. Unless you specifically give them leave to raise them, they may not for fear of appearing ignorant or uncertain. If towards the end of the goal-setting conversation, you ask if anything is unclear (the context or reason for the assignment, the QQTR, the ideal deliverable, etc.) you'll avoid miscommunication.

6. Assure mutual understanding

Lastly, to be doubly sure you and your team member have fully understood each other about what is to be done, re-

---

3 This idea comes from British business writer Andy Bounds' book, *The Jelly Effect*.
4 Ibid.

23

quest an oral summary. The celebrated British playwright George Bernard Shaw once said, "The single biggest problem in communication is the illusion that it has taken place."

You can check mutual understanding with a casual, respectful statement like, "Just so I am sure I gave you the assignment properly and didn't leave anything out, would you please recap it for me?" If your team member then repeats it back accurately, both of you will be confident you and your direct report are in sync.

> ❝
>
> **Our goals can only be reached through the vehicle of a plan, in which we must fervently believe, and upon which we must vigorously act. There is no other route to success."**
>
> – Pablo Picasso

After reading through this six-step assignment methodology, you may be thinking, "Who has time for all this?" But, the process is actually a time-saver. The clearer you are about what you want, the more focused your team members' efforts will be, the quicker the project will get done, and the better the deliverable. All that will remain is for everyone to celebrate the result.

If you consistently set goals, how much improvement in your team members' performance can you expect?

Researchers David E. Terpstra of the University of Mississippi and Elizabeth J. Rozell of Missouri Southern State College studied 200 firms that participated in a goal-setting survey.[5] Each company's HR Director responded positively or negatively to questions about whether managers in the organization used goal-setting. The researchers then correlated these responses with two financial measures: the one-year profit margin and the five-year profit growth.

Their results: Those firms that emphasized goal-setting enjoyed a 20% higher one-year profit margin and a 19% higher five-year growth rate. I'll bet you can achieve similar productivity improvements with your team.

Goal-setting clearly comes under The Universal Management Principle. By assigning realistic, challenging goals, you are promoting employee engagement, creating meaningful work, and giving your team members the opportunity to succeed. This shows you care. You will get back many times over what you have given.

---

5   David E. Terpstra and Elizabeth J. Rozell, "The Relationship of Goal-Setting to Organizational Profitability," *Group & Organization Management* 19, no. 3 (September 1994): 285-294.

Goal-Setting Challenge Questions

1. What are your most important goals?

_____
_____
_____
_____
_____
_____
_____

2. What are your most important goals you have set for your team members?

_____
_____
_____
_____
_____
_____
_____

3. Pick a goal that you will soon be assigning to a team member. Following the assignment-setting method in this chapter, write down how you will present this goal to this person?

_____
_____
_____
_____
_____
_____

Chapter 4

Rewards

One summer day, my high school best friend, Joe, and I had just finished playing three sets of tennis. Since Joe was captain of the varsity tennis team, I didn't have much of a chance to beat him. We had fun, though, and I was pleased to have given him a good game. The temperature was in the mid-eighties, and we were exhausted. We slouched down under a shady tree next to the court to relax, watching a group of track team members who, despite the heat, were doggedly jogging around the track surrounding the tennis courts.

"Imagine if we had to run three miles now?" I jokingly asked him.

"Well," he responded, with a quizzical expression that suggested he was weighing the possibilities, "I guess I could do it, if I had to."

"No way," I countered. I didn't think he could even get up. I decided to call his bluff. "Joe, I'll give you twenty dollars if you can do it." The next thing I knew, he had hoisted himself up, put on his cap and started lumbering toward the track. Forty-five minutes later, as I watched with increasing dread, he collapsed in triumph under the tree. "Thought I could do it," he said, putting out his hand to take my twenty, the last movement he would make for the next half-hour.

This was my first personal example of Expectancy Theory. This theory about the motivational value of rewards was developed by Victor Broom at the Yale School of Management. It has three parts:

1. The belief that one can perform a job or task successfully;

2. The confidence one has that successful completion will result in a reward;

3. The value one places on the reward.

In Joe's case, he believed he could run the three miles, he was confident I would pay him the twenty dollars, and he valued the money.

Another good example of Expectancy Theory is how team members respond when offered overtime. Those who volunteer are confident that they can do the work, sure that the company will pay them the stipulated time-and-a-half, and want the extra pay.

Here's how to apply this theory with your team to get similar extra effort.

Always encourage your team members to believe they will be successful. You want them to be like a winning sports team primed for the next game. Positive thinking is essential, especially your own.

Next, you want to reward your team members consistently for greater commitment and high achievement. Catch them doing things right and show your appreciation. A simple thank you is a good start, and we'll soon be discussing many other powerful rewards. The point is to reinforce your team members' extra effort so that they will continue to make it.

Lastly, tailor your rewards to what each person wants to the extent reasonably possible and without showing favoritism. Remember, the more a team member *values* the reward, the stronger his or her motivation will be.

This brings us to a discussion of what kinds of rewards work best. Rewards break down into two broad categories: extrinsic and intrinsic. Extrinsic rewards are those originating outside the individual, such as from his or her manager, from the company, or from an external source. Intrinsic rewards, on the other hand, are self-generated.

Extrinsic Rewards

The most obvious extrinsic reward is money. My friend, Joe, made this abundantly clear when he went after my

> **"**
> **The reward for work well done is the opportunity to do more."**
>
> – Jonas Salk, polio conqueror

twenty. In the workplace, how strong a motivator is money, i.e., compensation? The answer is nuanced. Research shows that for some employees it is indeed the primary motivator; for others, psychic rewards (intrinsic rewards) hold more sway.

Compensation as the primary motivator

For two kinds of team members, compensation is paramount: (a) those who need it to survive or to maintain a certain standard of living, and (b) those who view compensation as a measure of achievement and self-worth.

When I taught organizational behavior at Northeastern, I surveyed my students about what was most important to them in choosing their first full-time job. Was it how well they thought they would like the job, the boss they would work for, or how much they would earn? Their almost unanimous, immediate answer: "Money."

The simple reason was that they didn't have much. What they did have was student loans and the desire to live in an expensive city like Boston. My students reminded me of the truism that money is the number-one motivator when you need it. This is why minimum wage workers switch jobs so readily. Even an extra fifty cents or dollar an hour is meaningful. In our gig economy, many lower- and middle-income employees seek out multiple jobs for the same reason: they need the income.

Another compensation-driven group are employees who measure themselves by compensation, whose self-esteem rests on it. These team members are intensely competitive. They will go the extra mile for the extra dollar and will be very upset if they don't get it. No one works harder than a salesperson intent on reeling in the last order to reach a monthly sales goal. The opportunity to earn more through bonuses or contests energizes such individuals, and even small rewards like Starbucks gift cards can be motivating.[6]

In times when salaries are rising slowly, compensation seems to be especially important for job satisfaction, which is a primary energizer of motivation. The Society of Human Resources (SHRM) *2016 Employee Job Satisfaction and Engagement* study found that next to "Respectful treatment of all employees at all levels," compensation ranked the highest in contributing to job satisfaction:

At 63%, overall compensation/pay was the second most important contributor to job satisfaction, jumping from the fourth position in 2014. This aspect has held a spot within the leading five job satisfaction contributors since 2002.

Finally, financial incentives work especially well in motivating team members to do work that they dislike. If you need your team members to do something like making the work area sparkling clean to impress visitors, make it worth their while. Your offering to pay for beers or cocktails after work will get most team members hustling.

Money as a secondary motivator

> 66
>
> **People work for money but go the extra mile for recognition, praise and rewards."**
>
> – Dale Carnegie, motivational speaker and writer

---

6 Unfortunately, there is a downside to this almost compulsive behavior. Team members who are too compensation-driven may not always act ethically or in the best interests of the team or the organization.

29

Do team members who focus on compensation constitute the majority? In companies that adequately and fairly pay their employees, the answer is, "No."

According to the *Harvard Business Review* article, "Does Money Really Affect Motivation? A Review of the Research"[7]:

> We all need to pay our bills and provide for our families
>
> – but once these basic needs are covered, the psychological benefits of money are questionable.

The article author concludes that "120 years of research" and "92 quantitative studies" show:

> … the association between salary and job satisfaction is very weak.
>
> … people's satisfaction with their salary is mostly independent of their actual salary.
>
> …There is no significant difference in employee engagement by pay level.

In a nutshell, money does not buy engagement.

That money is a secondary motivator for the majority of fairly-paid team members makes sense when you consider the timing of raises and bonuses. Most companies review compensation only once a year. But motivation is a daily affair. If a team member knows his or her compensation is not going to change until the end of the year – and may depend on the fortunes of the entire company or department – is the team member really going to go all out every day?

To summarize, money is for most employees an important, but *not the most important*, motivator. The key point to remember is that compensation must be sufficient and fair.

Now, let us take a look at nonfinancial rewards. These can be very powerful, cost very little, and are only limited by a manager's imagination.

> **"**
>
> **Brains, like hearts, go where they are appreciated."**
>
> – Robert McNamara, former Secretary of Defense

---

7   Tomas Chamorro-Premuzic, "Does Money Really Affect Motivation? A Review of the Research," *Harvard Business Review*, April 10, 2013, https://hbr.org/2013/04/does-money-really-affect-motiv

Nonfinancial rewards

Tanya Tamay is the Vice President of Sales and Marketing for Organic Potage, a company that produces packaged soups like Heirloom Creamy Tomato, Free Range Chicken and Herbs, and Fresh Vegetable Medley. Her sales force sells primarily by telephone to large food brokers and supermarket chains.

In the common area outside her office stands a small replica of the Liberty Bell. When a team member makes a sale, he or she announces it by ringing the bell. The other team members then pop out of their cubicles to hear the good news. Clapping and congratulations follow. Bell-ringing happens at least every other day, and Tanya feels that these impromptu ceremonies are a welcome break and a morale booster.

Tanya especially loves to ring the bell to announce her own sales. On many late afternoons, her eyes on the clock, she is on the phone trying to nail a purchase order. She may need to reach a decision-maker on a business trip, negotiate away price issues, or resolve last-minute administrative snafus. She wants the reward of ringing the bell, sharing her excitement with her team members.

She has noticed, however, that some team members who also make noteworthy sales rarely ring the bell. The most common reason, she has discovered, is their discomfort with public recognition. The last thing they want is to have to make an announcement in front of the office staff and endure the back-slapping.

This example shows how differently two people can react to the same reward. You'll see team members perform to a much higher level, therefore, if you individualize rewards. You want to follow *The Platinum Rule*: "Treat others the way *they want to be treated*."

To ascertain what rewards will work best with your team members, try the following exercise with them:

Rewards for a Job Well Done

Consider this list of rewards for a job well done. **Identify the top three** that you would personally appreciate the most. Share and compare your answers with your team members and then **discuss the two questions** on the following page.

	Check Your Top 3
Handwritten thank-you note	
Announcement on social networking site, such as company's Facebook page	
Personal phone call from manager expressing appreciation	
Announcement on company web page	
Manager privately thanking you	
Email from company President	
Parking space closest to the building for one month	
Picture honoring your achievement on lobby bulletin board	
Text message from manager stating how wonderful you are	
Time off from work	
$100 gift card to restaurant or online retailer of your choice	
Lunch with manager	
Engraved plaque celebrating your achievement	
Small gift relating to something you value	
Recognition at team meeting	
Note sent to Human Resources noting your achievement	
Being named employee of the month	
Manager sending complimentary email to all team members	
$100 cash spot bonus	

Rewards for a Job Well Done

Discussion Questions

1. Did the other people in your group have different answers from yours?

2. What have you learned in completing this exercise?

I've tried this exercise on many employee groups, and it almost always shows how different people's reward preferences are. The important principle is:

Use the rewards that work best for each team member and for the team as a whole.

Based on your team's responses to the previous exercise, fill out the following table of which rewards are likely to be most meaningful and motivating to each of your direct reports. I've started you off with an example.

Individualizing Rewards for Maximum Motivation

Team member	Reward Ideas
Donald	Wants more overtime. Sparks to contests. Likes all forms of public recognition. Especially enjoys being called on in team meetings and sharing his expertise.

There is one reward that I'd now like to discuss in detail as research shows it is in a motivational class by itself.

Dr. Gerald Graham, a professor at Wichita State University, has been studying employee rewards since the 1980s. His standard research question is: "What motivates you to do your best?"

In one typical study[8] involving medical technologists, he found the top motivator to be "Manager personally congratulates employees who do a good job." In survey after survey with diverse employee groups, Dr. Graham has obtained similar results: personal recognition from a manager one likes and respects almost always emerges as number one.

You would therefore expect most managers to give recognition freely. In fact, in surveys, managers report that they do recognize their team members. If you ask your managerial colleagues, I'll bet almost all of them will agree that recognition is important and that they do it.

If you were to survey their team members, however, you would likely get a different story. What percentage of team members do you think *feel* they are recognized? Dr. Graham found that only 42% of them report that their managers frequently recognize their work. An article in the *Harvard Business Review* gives a percentage in the thirties.[9]

What managers say they do and what they actually do differ. Recognition, when it does occur, is often cursory. As John Hersey (see Chapter 1) points out, saying "Good job" becomes stale very quickly. A manager who never says much more is giving faint praise indeed.

To be meaningful, recognition has to be detailed and personalized (John Hersey calls it "Involved Recognition"). Common, frequently-used expressions like "awesome," "high five," or "go girl" can be applied to almost anyone about almost anything. Such trite phrases don't really touch the person. Over time, they lose whatever motivational power they may have originally held.

If a manager digs deeper to discover and praise the team member's unique contribution – including the financial benefits to the company – the congratulations make a greater impression. Team members appreciate managers who go to the trouble of finding out what they really did, their "special sauce" of extra effort and talent that has made their accomplishment noteworthy. Consider this example:

8 Gerald H. Graham and Jeanne Unruh, "The Motivational Impact of Nonfinancial Employee Appreciation Practices on Medical Technologists," *The Health Care Manager* 8, no. 3 (April 1990): 9-18.

9 Lou Solomon, "The Top Complaints from Employees About Their Leaders," *Harvard Business Review*, June 24, 2015, https://hbr.org/2015/06/the-top-complaints-from-employees-about-their-leaders

Jack Ryan is the Controller of Starfire Entertainment Inc., a casino builder and operator. Starfire's latest project is a dazzling new entertainment and hotel complex on the site of a failed casino in Atlantic City.

As the casino will open in three months, Jack is soliciting vendor bids for 3,000 slot machines. Just as the bids are starting to come in, he gets the flu and has to go home to rest. He emails his Assistant Controller, Nancy Armada, to please review the bids. Within a week, Jack must decide which vendor to buy from, or the casino opening may be delayed.

Three days later, Jack, still sick, drags himself into the office, ready to pull together the comparative analysis. Jack is delighted to discover that Nancy has gathered all the relevant quotes. What's more, using the same spreadsheet he had developed for similar cost comparisons, she has already put in the vendor pricing and made a recommendation. The analysis is done!

What makes Nancy's work so special, Jack sees, is that she has itemized each vendor's bid to make the quotes directly comparable. How, Jack wonders, did she get this detailed pricing information? In addition, she has added some charts and "bells and whistles" making his spreadsheet look great. In short, she

has done everything except tie a ribbon around this project.

Not only is Jack excited about Nancy's work, he realizes that she is ready to take on increasingly sophisticated projects in the future, allowing him to focus on strategic initiatives.

If all that Jack does to recognize Nancy's extraordinary work is to say, "Nancy, excellent job; thanks a lot," she will likely be pleased but not all that excited. In fact, her reaction may be, "I nearly killed myself on this project. Surely Jack can say more than these clichés."

Jack does understand and appreciate what a wonderful job Nancy has done. He just hasn't told her. To recognize her fully, he needs to research exactly what Nancy did. He will be pleased to discover that she interviewed each vendor to get the detailed bid breakdown.

With this preparation, Jack might then call Nancy into his office and say something more meaningful, such as: "Nancy, you have done a wonderful job. What I especially like is that you contacted each vendor to get the revised, uniform bids. Your apples-to-apples comparative data really allowed me to see what each vendor was charging. I might have gone with Ace Slots if your spreadsheet had not shown their ongoing maintenance charges to be so high. Your detailed analysis took the guesswork out of the project.

"I'll tell you something else. As you know, the casino opening day schedule is tight. I think, based on your presentation, I can get the slot machine order out early. This means we'll receive the machines on the casino floor several days before we had planned to, and our engineers can properly calibrate them. By opening day, I bet all the machines, instead of our usual 80%, will be operational. The benefit of this will be thousands of dollars in extra revenue. And that's just terrific – all the result of your extra effort." (Jack might even back up his words with a spot bonus.)

How do you think Nancy will feel after Jack recognizes her in this manner? What do you think she'll say when she comes home that evening and her partner asks, "How was your day?" She'll most likely radiate pride as she reports her manager's glowing review. Most importantly, to earn additional recognition, she will look to take on even more difficult projects in the future, just as Jack had hoped.

While a one-on-one conversation is almost always a desirable way to recognize a team member, public recognition at team meetings can work well, too, pro-viding (a) the team member is comfortable with it and (b) there are frequent opportunities for such public recognition so that all deserving team members can be similarly praised.

Intrinsic motivation

Now, let's consider team members who are driven primarily by *intrinsic motivation,* who simply feel pride in their work and a duty to do it well. Their reward mechanism is similar to the one discussed earlier in this chapter. They believe that they can do their jobs well, that they will be rewarded – in this case, through feelings of self-satisfaction – and that such rewards are meaningful to them. How can you provide extra motivation to these committed team members who just plain *enjoy what they do*?

The answer is: Provide them with the right tools and support, and *let them fly.*

Dr. Harry Levinson (1922 – 2012), a famed psychologist and management consultant who first applied psychoanalytic concepts to the workplace, explained why this is so important. Levinson theorized that employees recognize and remember highly gratifying work experiences that intimately fit their personalities. As they progress in their careers, they discover when they feel their best at work and what types of tasks they particularly enjoy. Levinson called this internal awareness the "ego ideal." He concluded that work closely tied to the ego ideal is inherently motivating.

If you, as a concerned manager, take the time to learn what your team members really want to do and how they want to develop, you'll discover how to harness their natural motivation. (Keep in mind what motivates you will not necessarily motivate them.) As I have said, all intrinsically-motivated team members need to perform at their best is work that excites them and the proper resources and support to do it.

Exercising this kind of thoughtful leadership is yet another example of applying The Universal Management Principle. How many managers have you ever worked for who went out of their way to give you work that floated your boat? I'll bet the ones who did are the managers you liked and respected the most -- and for whom you worked the hardest.

Rewards Challenge Questions

1. Which of your team members are primarily motivated by compensation, awards, or prizes? Which ones respond well to personalized or group recognition? Which ones are intrinsically-motivated?

   _____

   _____

   _____

   _____

   _____

   _____

2. Given the above answers, what might you do to improve the rewards, recognition, or support you offer to your team members to better motivate them?

   _____

   _____

   _____

   _____

   _____

   _____

3. Try out personalized recognition (as described in this chapter) on one of your team members who has recently accomplished something important. What was the result?

   _____

   _____

   _____

   _____

   _____

   _____

Chapter 5

Job Enrichment

Have you ever worked at a job you truly loved? If so, you are fortunate, and this chapter should resonate with you. Alternatively, if you are not happy at work, this chapter may help you understand clearly the reasons for your dissatisfaction. Most importantly, this chapter will help you design team member jobs that are fully engaging.

Up to now, I've presented motivational techniques that a good manager should do like granting autonomy, setting goals, and giving rewards. But, wouldn't motivating your team be easier if each team member's job came with *motivation built right in?* Let's take a look at seven job design factors that can produce this result.

The first five relate to what organizational behavior researchers call the Job Characteristics Model developed by J. Richard Hackman and Greg Oldham in the 1970s. Over 200 studies support its validity.[10] The last two factors are ones I have added as they are obviously important to include.

Seven Job Design Factors that Motivate Team Members

1. *Skill Variety* – the scope of skills the job requires;

2. *Task Identity* – responsibility for the entire job or a significant portion of it;

3. *Task Significance* – the positive meaning or purpose behind the work and its impact on others;

4. *Autonomy* – the independence and discretion the job allows (see Chapter 1);

5. *Feedback* – how much information is given on work performance and results achieved;

6. *Social Connection* – whether or not the work promotes positive relationships with other employees, vendors, community representatives, and/or customers.

7. *Rewards* – the benefits received for a job well done and how much they are valued (see Chapter 4).

To illustrate how a manager can design a job that has these factors and is inherently motivating, consider the example of Tamara Jones who manages a claims processing team at a leading home property insurer. Here is a job design chart her boss created:

---

10 Cristina B. Gibson *et al.*, "Including the 'I' in Virtuality and Modern Job Design: Extending the Job Characteristics Model to Include the Moderating Effect of Individual Experiences of Electronic Dependence and Copresence," *Organization Science* 22, no. 6 (November-December 2011): 1481-1499.

Seven Desirable Job Factors	Tamara Jones, Customer Service Team Leader
1. *Skill variety*	Handles a wide variety of home insurance loss claims, trains junior staff, and participates in cross-functional teams.
2. *Task Identity*	Has responsibility for customer claims from initial call to adjuster report to final reimbursement. Reviews customer satisfaction questionnaires for customers she has serviced.
3. *Task Significance*	"Our customers are our business." Tamara knows this and feels the importance of her responsibilities. She has said she is proud of helping people in crisis who depend on her for prompt, satisfactory claim resolution. "Some of my clients become like family," she has said.
4. *Autonomy*	Within guidelines, Tamara can do whatever she decides is necessary to resolve customer claims. She can also escalate issues or propose new policies.
5. *Feedback*	Receives individual monthly review and mentoring session, participates in weekly staff meetings and attends problem-solving "lunch and learns."
6. *Social Connection*	She can consult with other team members to problem-solve in real time. She likes our open office design that promotes social interaction. Attends training classes regularly. Tamara is a leader in the "Diverse Interns" program. She helps plan the Christmas party and participates in other company events.
7. *Reward*	Has received three raises since joining company two years ago. Salary package is fully competitive. Has gotten individualized recognition twice in the last two months. Received company "Top Leader" award for "Diverse Interns" program.

To evaluate your team members' jobs, fill out a similar chart for each of them.

Even if a manager has the best of intentions, sometimes the reality of a job can stray from its original design. Consider this example illustrating a worst case situation:

Brian Byers came from a small town in western Pennsylvania and had always dreamed of working as a nurse in a large city like Boston, home to so many prestigious research and teaching hospitals. After receiving his RN degree from Northeastern University, he did additional training in general nursing at Mass General and Beth Israel hospitals before accepting a full-time position at Patriot Hospital. He was particularly impressed by this hospital's pioneering research in transplant immunosuppression and looked forward to eventually joining the transplant team.

Here is an excerpt from the original job description that enticed him to accept the position.

Registered Nurse Job Responsibilities

- Track patient's condition and fully meet needs to provide the best possible nursing care (*Task Identity, Task Significance, Social Connection*)

- Observe patient's symptoms and assess test results, communicating them to the physician medical team (*Task Significance, Social Connection*)

- Provide immediate medical attention in emergencies (*Skill Variety, Task Identity, Task Significance, Autonomy*)

- Supervise and train Certified Nurse Assistants (*Skill Variety, Task Identity, Task Significance, Social Connection*)

- Foster a caring and concerned environment for patients and their families (*Task Significance, Social Connection*)

- Participate as part of the medical team to review treatment plans, attend rounds and receive training (*Feedback*)

Doesn't this job description sound appealing? Brian soon discovered, however, that the actual job was far different. Brian had walked into a hornet's nest of labor unrest.

"

You've got to love what you do to really make things happen."

– Philip Green, Chairman, Arcadia Group

The same year Brian came aboard, Patriot Hospital reported a $2.6 million loss. Patriot's senior management was forced to seek labor economies. The cost-cutting fell heavily on the nursing staff. Brian soon had responsibility for so many patients that he felt he could not do a thorough job with any of them.

To complicate matters, on a daily basis he got text messages offering him a chance to pick up night shifts due to the nursing shortage. With his student loan burden, he found himself tempted to accept them, but when he did, he found he was exhausted the next day.

What bothered Brian the most was the risk to patient health. RNs were all too often filling in on units where they had little experience or training in specialized procedures.

One day, he looked at his original job description and realized that it was full of empty promises. Brian gladly joined other nurses at Patriot Hospital in an historic strike over patient safety, working conditions, and compensation. While the strike was a short one, by the time it was over, Brian, like many of his young fellow nurses, had become disillusioned with Patriot's leadership. He soon left for a new position at Mass General Hospital.

Brian's story shows how quickly team member jobs can take a turn for the worse. If this might be happening with your team, make corrective changes as soon as you can. Even if you don't succeed, your team members will appreciate the effort that you have made and the caring that you have demonstrated. They will continue to try their best.

> **To win in the marketplace you must first win in the workplace."**
>
> – Douglas Conant, former CEO of Campbell Soup

As you might suspect, poor job design is all too common. Most organizations look to employees to do what management wants and forget about what employees need. Employees become stressed out or discouraged. They may just go through the motions. Consider these study results:

The SHRM *2016 Employee Job Satisfaction and Engagement study* mentioned in Chapter 4 found that the average team member was only moderately engaged at work. On a scale of 1 to 5, the employee engagement statistic was 3.7.

In a very large Gallup study (195,000 employees) done in 2015-2016 – *State of the*

American Workplace – only one-third of employees reported that they were engaged at work. In fact, "The majority of employees (51%) are not engaged and haven't been for quite some time."[11] The motivation problem, the study shows, is acute in larger organizations and among lower level employees.

The good news is that the best organizations, those that offer employees meaningful work and pay close attention to their job satisfaction, have higher rates of employee engagement and, as a consequence, are *much more profitable*. In a study[12] which compared Fortune magazine's "Best Places to Work" with matched, comparable companies, the best companies had an average 28% higher return on assets over six years.

If you design and maintain team member jobs according to the seven desirable job factors, consulting periodically the chart you created earlier, your team members will naturally have high morale, be consistently motivated, and produce superior results. With your having such an engaged team, your own job will be a lot easier and more enjoyable, too.

> **"**
>
> **If you want people to do a good job, give them a good job to do — an enriched job."**
>
> – Frederick Hertzberg, American psychologist

---

11 Gallup, *State of the American Workplace*, 2017 edition.

12 "Are the 100 Best Better? An Empirical Investigation of the Relationship Between Being a 'Great Place to Work' and Firm Performance," *Personnel Psychology*, Winter 2003.

Chapter 6

Fairness

MagicView is a software company in Chicago. Its main product is a web-based document viewer that instantly displays any type of file. No other software, such as Microsoft Office or Adobe Acrobat, is necessary. For organizations like banks and insurance companies that receive thousands of diverse files and images every day, MagicView's viewer is an indispensable business tool.

Karen Steele, thirty-six years old, is the company's customer service manager. She has worked for MagicView for five years. As she and her staff solve thorny customer service issues, they sometimes learn about new sales opportunities. A customer might inquire, for example, "Can MagicView integrate the document archive of our new subsidiary?" Karen usually handles such requests by delving deeply into them to be sure MagicView offers the right solution. She then talks up MagicView's capabilities before personally introducing her customer to the appropriate MagicView sales representative.

One day, Karen heard one of them bragging to a colleague about the high sales commission he had just received.

"I didn't even have to do anything to make the sale, actually. Karen Steele brought the customer right to me. I talked with the prospect to confirm what Karen had said, and the purchase order came in the very next day. *Sweet.*"

Karen felt anger surge through her. She was the one really responsible for the sale. Yet she had received nothing for it, not even a thank you.

After she had calmed down, Karen went to see MagicView's VP of Sales and Marketing, Jose Almado, pointing out to him the injustice. She explained that this had happened several times before; her team was always referring sales opportunities. "In fact," she concluded, "you really could say our department is generating its share of new business. I know this is all part of our jobs, but still, don't we deserve some financial reward?"

"Karen," Jose responded, with a smile of understanding and resignation, "you know that's the way it works around here. If you want to make commission, you have to be in sales. It is not company policy to pay incentives to customer service people."

After Karen had left his office, Jose, a twenty-year company veteran, ruminated about what she had said. Perhaps she had a point. But thinking about Karen's dilemma soon led him to reflect on his own feelings of injustice. He was a key member of the management team, which consisted of MagicView's owners, a brother-and-sister team (Chief Software Engineer and CEO, respectively), the sister's son (Controller), fresh out of business school, a newly-hired Senior HR Director, and himself. This group met once a week to chart the company's course.

Everyone on the team was supposed to work cooperatively The CEO often said, "We are successful because we listen to and respect each other." Lately, this process had broken down. The brother and sister were increasingly fighting. Neither one was interested in listening to Jose, who tried to play a peacemaker role. Furthermore, as VP of Sales and Marketing, he felt his views should be more thoughtfully considered. After all, the company had achieved an average 10% yearly sales growth under his watch.

Now, too many decisions were bitter compromises and often, he felt, not in the company's long-term best interests. Jose worried that the its growth rate would stall, limiting opportunity for loyal employees like himself and many others.

Lixuan Chan, the HR head and the most experienced management team member, found the management meetings

> ## 66
> **To handle yourself, use your head. To handle others, use your heart."**
>
> – Eleanor Roosevelt

equally disturbing. When she had been hired, the CEO emphasized her collegial management style and how welcome Lixuan's input would be. The reality was that when Lixuan spoke up, the two owners treated her like a junior employee who needed to learn how the company *really* worked. They rarely sought out her opinion before making major HR decisions. She had been hired to turn what was still a family business into a professionally-structured organization but had had little opportunity to do so. She was profoundly disappointed.

Less than a year after Karen Steele had voiced her frustrations to Jose Almado, she left MagicView to become Customer Service Director at another firm offering a company-wide bonus plan. A third of her staff went with her.

Jose Almado is also no longer with MagicView. A headhunter, whom he had avoided in the past, recruited him for a VP of Sales and Marketing position at a well-funded startup.

Lixuan Chan decided to start her own HR consultancy. She found that a surprising number of clients were willing to listen to her and pay handsomely for her advice.

Isn't it obvious why Karen, Jose, and Lixuan left at the same time? They were treated unfairly, events came to a head, and they became so angry they decided to move on.

MagicView's sibling owners, as a result of the above defections and their own continuing troubled relationship, put the company up for sale. They received only a few disappointing offers. Potential acquirers liked the company's excellent software and growth trajectory, but judged its hastily-reconstituted management team as weak and unproven. The owners' conduct had cost them millions of dollars.

This example illustrates how crucial it can be to treat employees, or anyone, fairly. The desire for fair treatment runs deep in all of us. Research shows that humans display a sense of fairness that almost no other species, including our closest relatives, chimpanzees, exhibits.[13] If you have children, you know that by age eight they understand the concept, especially when they feel they are not getting what they deserve. (If you don't believe me, put two second graders together and offer only one a chocolate-chip cookie.)

In the employer/employee relationship, expectations of fair treatment on both sides start right from the hiring handshake. Dr. Harry Levinson, whom we

mentioned in the chapter on rewards, and other social scientists have called this the "psychological contract."

Levinson defined it as an unwritten agreement based upon mutual expectations as to how the company (and especially, the employee's manager) will treat the employee and how the employee, in return, will perform. If the job meets the new employee's expectations, his motivation stays high. If not, the employee feels betrayed, and his motivation sinks. Team members may even retaliate or, like MagicView's three staffers and Brian Byers in the previous chapter, leave.

How can you as a manager be sure that your team members feel fairly treated?

Fairness is always based upon a comparison. Stephen Hawking, the celebrated British physicist who struggled with Lou Gehrig's disease, for example, rarely felt sorry for himself despite being confined to a wheelchair and eventually becoming unable to speak or type without assistance. He always remembered a boy who was dying of leukemia in the hospital bed next to him while Dr. Hawking was undergoing a medical test.

"Clearly there were people worse off than me," he was quoted in the *Boston Globe*[14] as saying. "At least my condition didn't make me feel sick. Whenever I feel

13   Kerri Smith, "Children Learn Rules of Equality by Age Eight," *Nature*, August 27, 2008, doi:10.1038/news.2008.1064
14   Mark Feeney, "Stephen Hawking, 76, ground-breaking Physicist," *Boston Globe*, March 14, 2018.

49

inclined to be sorry for myself, I remember that boy."

While Dr. Hawking consoled himself with a comparison that made his situation seem more favorable, comparisons at work usually go in the opposite direction. There are so many ways a team member can feel unfairly treated. He can compare his previous job with his present one. He can ask a friend at another company how things work there. He can contrast his pay with that of a co-worker. He can feel betrayed when management does not behave ethically or live up to its traditional values. He may get a new manager who is unaware and unappreciative of his past contributions and achievements, etc. [15]

In general, employees' perceptions of unfair treatment break down into four categories:

1. *Rewards* – who gets which rewards, and how much;

2. *Processes* – the way management makes decisions or establishes policies;

3. *Relationships* – how employees are treated and how they are communicated with;

> ❝
> **Fairness Is not an attitude. It's a professional Skill That Must Be Developed And Exercised."**
>
> – Brit Hume, American television journalist

4. *Organization* – the company's culture and ethical values.

With these multiple pitfalls – and how sensitive some employees are! – you might think a manager should just treat everyone equally. But this approach doesn't work very well. In fact, team members don't like it. Many successful sports teams, for example, pay their star players more – sometimes a lot more – than their average ones. Yet these teams perform better with this talent on board and generate higher team spirit than those teams that have flat compensation and do poorly. Team members usually understand that differences in talent and experience justify compensation and treatment disparities.

Team members will also accept a certain amount of unfairness resulting from company politics, arbitrary decisions, and indifferent management. They know all organizations have these problems. Each employee, however, has a fairness "red line" that should not be crossed. Management risks torpedoing employee motivation by a single unfair act or policy that goes over it.

---

15 As Theodore Roosevelt also said, "Comparison is the thief of joy."

In March of 2018, for instance, United Airlines announced that it would replace a monthly performance incentive plan for its 80,000 employees with a prize lottery.[16] Workers with perfect attendance for the month would be eligible for a random drawing with a top cash prize of $100,000. Other prizes included a Mercedes C-Class car, luxury vacations, and $2,000 in cash for up to a thousand workers.

" Employees seem to have a general concern for fairness that transcends the self."

– Deborah Rupp, industrial-organizational psychologist

While these prizes seem lavish, in truth the company would be saving tens of millions of dollars a year. According to the *New York Times* article, United Airlines paid "approximately $87 million in earned bonuses in 2017."

Employees were up in arms. In an online petition, one worker characterized the new replacement lottery as "unfair and unjust." The number of employees who would qualify for the new plan would be much smaller than the old one. As one worker put it:

> "When no one 'qualifies' because they called out sick due to the most awful flu in years or sick children, or life … the company just makes more money for itself. Service is going to lack, on-time departures won't be fought for and the company will suffer."[17]

You have probably experienced several examples of unfair treatment yourself. Remember how angrily you reacted? If you see or suspect that one of your team members is feeling unfairly treated and you are in a position to take corrective action, be sure to do so. Start with a frank discussion to get to the bottom of the team member's concerns. Be ready to take any heartfelt criticism or expressions of frustration. Get everything out in the open. (Having the courage to conduct such a sensitive conversation really shows you care and is thus an example of The Universal Management Principle.)

Once your team member's emotions have been sufficiently dealt with, you can discuss corrective action. If the source of the unfairness cannot be remedied, Plan B is to explain the situation as best you can. Try to give a good reason why a par-

---

16 Christina Caron, "United Rethinks Plan to Replace Workers' Bonuses With a Big-Prize Lottery," *New York Times,* March 6, 2018.

17 Ibid.

ticular action has been taken. You'll get a better result, studies show[18], if you can give a legitimate excuse – an explanation – rather than a justification. What's the difference?

Suppose there is a company-wide staff reduction, and a manager has to lay off a team member. The manager chooses the person who, in her view, is the weakest contributor to the team. After the layoff, she calls a team meeting to explain her action (if she fails to do this, all kinds of rumors will sprout). Which of the following speeches is likely to go over better?

1. "There is a mandated 10 percent staff reduction in the company due to our sales shortfall this year. I had no choice but to lay off one of our team."

2. "Harry was let go because I felt we really don't need him. If we all pitch in, we won't miss him."

The first is an explanation that is easily understood and reasonable given the company's current downturn. The manager clarifies her intentions in a way that will likely deflect team member anger. The second is a justification. The manager's saying Harry's leaving won't make a difference anyway smacks of something concocted after the fact. Team members may wonder what hurtful actions she may take next.

To sum up this chapter's lesson, fairness provides the foundation for motivation. If a manager, or a company, fails to treat team members fairly, none of this book's motivational techniques will work very well. Fairness is an elemental expression of caring and, as such, central to The Universal Management Principle.

---

18   John C. Shaw, Eric Wild, and Jason A. Colquitt, "To Justify or Excuse?" *Journal of Applied Psychology* 88, no. 3 (2003): 444-458.

Fairness Challenge Questions

1. During the last six months, has your company acted unfairly to any of its employees? What was the result?

_____

_____

_____

_____

_____

_____

_____

2. If you have inadvertently treated any of your team members unfairly, how can you best remedy this situation?

_____

_____

_____

_____

_____

_____

_____

3. If you've had to recently let a team member go or take other adverse action, did you communicate the reasons to your team? Did you give a legitimate excuse or explanation, or did you just offer a justification?

_____

_____

_____

_____

_____

_____

Chapter 7

Transformational Leadership

In the face of changing circumstances and to take advantage of new opportunities, a smart manager needs to become a transformational leader. A transformational leader conceives a brighter future for her team or company and leads the way to realizing it.

The threat of adverse change is always on the horizon: The market may move in a new direction; operations that are going well may falter; a key employee may leave; competitors may launch an unexpected attack; a new, disruptive technology may arise.

It is the suddenness with which change sometimes occurs that is so damaging. The taxi industry in New York City, for example, was quickly decimated by the rise of ride-sharing services. DVD rental businesses disappeared when video streaming took hold, and cable TV monopolies face an upswell of cord cutting millennials.

Perhaps you have already started down the transformational leadership path? You can see by answering the following questions:

Question	Yes	No
1. If you were asked, "What is your vision for your team's (or your company's) future success?" would you have a ready answer?		
2. Have you written your vision down?		
If you answered "Yes" to both of these questions, proceed.		
3. Have you started to think about a game plan to realize your vision?		
4. Are you already planning any necessary changes to your team's structure, job assignments, or business practices?		
5. Have you started actively communicating your vision to your team through personal appeals, team meetings, emails, and other channels?		

6. Are you modelling the attitudinal or behavioral changes appropriate to your vision? Honestly, are you "walking the talk"?		
7. Do you believe that your team and others in your company respect you sufficiently to carry out your vision?		
8. Have you consulted with your team members and asked them to contribute their ideas?		
9. Do you regularly meet one-on-one with each of your team members to support, help, or encourage him or her?		
10. Are you prepared to take action against team members who may resist implementing your vision?		

If you answered "Yes" to both questions 1 and 2, and if you answered "Yes" to at least half the questions that followed, you are well on your way to becoming a transformational leader.

To define more concretely what a transformational leader does, we can turn to the work of researcher Bernard M. Bass, who, along with other investigators, characterized a transformational leader's skillset as:

1. Creating an inspiring vision for the team's, or the company's, future success;

2. Crafting a game plan to execute the vision;

3. Stimulating team members' innovative thinking, diverse opinions, and conflicting ideas;

4. Exhibiting admirable personal qualities that engender team member support;

5. Caring about individual team members and relating warmly and intensely to them.

Let's examine these traits.

Creating an inspiring vision for the team's, or the company's, future success

When we think about vision, well-known figures like Steve Jobs, Melinda Gates, or Elon Musk may come to mind. Any implied comparison may be daunting. You may be thinking, "How can I do the kinds of things these luminaries have done?" Because they have exceptional abilities and resources, you likely can't.

Yet, *you can be a visionary in your own way.* How can you do this? According to 19th-century German philosopher Arthur Schopenhauer, "The task is not so much to see what no one has seen yet, but to think what nobody has thought yet about what everybody sees."

Schopenhauer is asking us to think creatively about what is right in front of our noses. The majority of organizational innovations (in my opinion) are pretty straightforward. Someone gets an idea that if a home toothbrush rotated like the one the dental hygienist uses, it would clean more thoroughly. An aspiring entrepreneur asks, "Wouldn't it be cool to be able to find a deeply discounted hotel room the same day you need it?" Consumer research reveals people wish they had a home robot vacuum cleaner that scoots around.

My point is most thoughtful managers can develop a vision if they put their mind to it. Some companies, like large pharmaceutical firms, institutionalize this type of focused, forward-looking thinking. Their R&D labs periodically create breakthrough drugs by routinely analyzing soil samples and other readily-available organic material.

> ❝
>
> **Optimism isn't a passive conviction that things will get better; it's a conviction that we can make things better."**
>
> – Melinda Gates

To develop a vision for your team, ask, "What should be changed? Where are we at risk? Where is the market going? What should we be doing differently? Where does opportunity lie?" You don't have to be a "visionary" to answer such questions. You just need to be curious, open to change, and committed to creating a better future.

One day in 1960, Bruce Goecker of Novato, CA found that he was tired of struggling to commute back and forth to work every day across the Golden Gate Bridge between Marin County and San Francisco. The problem was the backup at the toll booths going in each direction. He had a simple idea: why not let commuters drive in free in the morning and then charge a double toll on the way home? After all, the same people who drove in would return at night. This would cut traffic jams in half.

Goecker began a one-person campaign that took eight years to convince the Golden Gate Bridge Authority to give the new method a try. On October 19, 1968, the test began, and he was given the honor of being the first to cross in the free inbound direction. The one-way toll did indeed reduce morning traffic congestion without otherwise affecting the outbound flow. Eventually, almost all bridges in California – and many across the country – switched to one-way tolls, with equally beneficial results.

In the late 1970's, a young couple, Dan and Hilary Fylstra, started Personal Software, a small company in Allston, MA, to develop software for the early hobbyist personal computers. Personal Software's first products were computer games, including one of the earliest chess-playing programs, MicroChess.

At the time, Dan was a student at Harvard Business School, focusing on marketing. So when another student, Dan Bricklin, came to him with an idea for a business-related program, Dan Fylstra was interested. He proposed that the program should be written for a new computer, the Apple II. The program created an on-screen grid into which a user could input numbers and formulas. The program could then compute and display the numbers, updating the entire grid. The user could make as many changes as desired – the program was magical.

The business opportunity that Dan Fylstra foresaw lay in the combination of this new software, Apple II as the hardware, and computer stores for sales and support.

VisiCalc, as Dan named the program, was the first spreadsheet and ushered in the personal computer revolution in business. "If VisiCalc had been written for some other computer," Apple co-founder Steve Jobs told a television interviewer in 1990, "you'd be interviewing somebody else right now."[19]

Personal Software (soon renamed Visi-Corp) grew to 120 employees and over $40 million in sales before it yielded spreadsheet market leadership to Lotus 1-2-3 and Microsoft Excel. My point is that a transformational leader like Dan Fylstra, running a small company, can dramatically change the world and his firm's destiny.

Remember, if you don't have a vision, your team will simply continue on its present course. "We've always done it this way" is an all too common refrain.

Crafting a game plan to execute the vision and *Stimulating team members' innovative thinking, diverse opinions, and conflicting ideas*

Next, ask yourself what major organizational or structural changes will be necessary to turn your vision into a reality. Research shows that such "big picture" moves will have a large impact on your team's results.[20] You may need to reorganize your team or company, reserve funds for capital equipment, contract

19 Scott Kirsner, "They Were the Wizards of '78," *Boston Globe*, February 2, 2018.
20 Robert T. Keller, "Transformational Leadership, Initiating Structure, and Substitutes for Leadership," *Journal of Applied Psychology* 91, no. 1 (2005): 202-210.

for outside services, etc. (Managers commonly think an expansion starts with hiring the right people; in many situations, it starts with finding the office space to house them.) For any or all of these reasons, *get started planning early and focus on the big picture*.

Once you have fleshed out your vision, gather your team together to explain it and to ask for everyone's help in developing an execution game plan. If you conduct this meeting off-premises – as a retreat, for example – you will further emphasize its importance. Bringing in a facilitator may make the meeting even more productive. Over several hours, encourage active discussion, remaining open to hearing your team members' ideas and getting their input. You may be the leader, but many heads are surely better than one. Encourage conflicting points of view. A certain amount of creative chaos is a good way to start.

Anticipate opposition or skepticism. If your team members look at you with a "*Huh*?" expression, that's a good sign; you've likely got an excellent idea. As Schopenhauer also reminds us, "All truth passes through three stages. First, it is ridiculed. Second, it is violently opposed. Third, it is accepted as being self-evident."

On the other hand, if your team members tell you right away, "Yeah, that's a great idea," most likely, it isn't. A competitor has already thought of it or, upon further analysis, you'll discover you've been carried away by your enthusiasms.

Let me emphasize that full involvement of your team is essential. When you are the only one who does the thinking or makes the decisions, your team members will become dependent on you. They will shy away from taking the initiative. Talented ones may even leave for jobs with greater autonomy or to work for companies that value their input. The more involved your team is in formulating the plan, the more committed they will be to executing it. It is the troops on the ground that take the hill.

The next story shows how beneficial this team member interaction can be.

Susan Jones owns a company, Lovable Grains, that makes granola from a recipe she created. Her unique mix of dried cranberries and blueberries, rolled oats, ancient grains, and maple sugar has

> ❝
> **A genuine leader is not a searcher for consensus but a molder of consensus."**
>
> – Dr. Martin Luther King, Jr.

made "Artisan Organic Granola" a supermarket staple.

Susan's company freshens its granola packaging design each year. For the first couple of years, Susan simply came up with the new design herself. Then, one year, her team appeared skeptical when she presented the next year's mock-up. "Susan, with all due respect," one team member pointed out, "that design really isn't new. Instead of just using type, why don't we switch to a picture – say, of an organic farm?" Another commented, "Let's also change the font from 'folksy' to one that pops." Suddenly, the team was off and running, brainstorming many wonderful, innovative packaging concepts.

Susan immediately saw the value of this creative process. The design would surely be better, her staff's excitement about her company's flagship product would be contagious, and Lovable Grains' distributors would catch the wave. As the meeting ended, Susan experienced a rush of personal humility and pride in her team's wonderful work.

Once you and your team have come together on the vision game plan, write it down. I recommend a chart with the following columns:

a. A vision statement that all team members sign on to;

b. Game plan goals;

c. Step-by-step implementation assignments with team member responsibilities and deadlines;

d. Interim and final benchmarks;

e. Ground rules as to how team members will communicate and support each other during the execution process; (This step is commonly omitted or given short shrift, but it is very important);

f. Rewards that team members will receive for successful game plan execution.

Here is an illustration of a fictional sports drink company's game plan for the launch of Nature Juice, "the energy drink of Incan warriors."

Nature Juice Game Plan Worksheet

Succinct Vision Statement	Game Plan Goals	Team Member Assignments	Benchmarks	How the Team will Communicate and Support Each Other	Rewards
To introduce the new sports drink, "Nature Juice, the energy beverage of Peru's historic Incan Warriors," in selected US markets	City-wide sales displays in convenience stores and supermarkets in twelve major metro markets A minimum of three national sports figure endorsements 10 major sports event sponsorships Publicity releases and local television news stories in all target markets June 1 launch with simultaneous publicity, TV spots, sampling, and store displays	Mary: meet with regional distributors to sell launch plan and marshal their support Sandy: issue publicity releases and produce TV video clips David: contact sports agents for client endorsements Tasha: create college sampling program and point-of-purchase displays Joan: have signed distribution agreements in place in all target markets Brian: have sufficient cases of Nature Juice in three flavors ready to ship two weeks before launch date	Three athletes signed by March 15 Distributor contracts by April 1 Publicity releases ready and videos produced by May 1 Product in warehouse by May 15.	Weekly email updates, one-on-one informal meetings, and monthly group meetings (dates attached)	June 15 launch party for the team $5,000 per team member incentive bonus if test results in nationwide rollout

In laying out such a chart for your team's game plan, be careful to establish clear accountabilities. You will want to carefully monitor team member assignments, benchmarks, and deadlines. You should also continually communicate your team's progress through periodic announcements, meetings, and emails. Remember, *you can never communicate too much*. If you like the idea of ringing the bell for each benchmark completion (see "Chapter 4 – Rewards") get yourself one.

Next, make sure that you, as the transformational leader, are personally involved in the toughest tasks. For example, if your game plan includes finding a new national distributor, make the introductory calls yourself. If your company needs a state law variance, assign yourself the job of contacting state representatives. Always lead from the front; you'll find your team members lining up right behind you.

Since innovation almost always generates resistance, you will also have to make sure team members are fully on board and moving ahead with their individual assignments. A good way to do this is to set up periodic individual team member check-ins. Conduct what I call

"3x3x3" meetings: Ask each team member to come prepared with three things that are going well for them, three things that are not going well, and three things of their own choosing — all related to the game plan's execution.

The first 3x3x3 meeting may be tense as team members will not know what to expect, but you'll soon see that they welcome them as a regular opportunity to share their concerns and update you on their progress. With your help, you may find a troubling issue raised in one month's 3x3x3 meeting will become a success story in the next.

> **"**
> **Leadership is the capacity to translate vision into reality."**
>
> – Warren Bennis,
> organizational consultant

These meetings will also demonstrate to your team members that you care about them, applaud their efforts, and believe in their abilities.

If, despite your best coaching efforts, you find a team member is holding back, take corrective action. You can try counseling. If this doesn't work, make it clear you won't tolerate opposition. As a last resort, remove the team member from the team. Always display conviction that team members must perform, and that with everyone pulling together, the game plan will succeed.

Exhibiting admirable personal qualities that engender team member support

When team members respect you, they are likely to go all out to achieving the game plan's objectives. Team members closely observe their leader's behavior. A leader's support of an admirable purpose or principle is particularly inspiring, as illustrated in this next installment of the Lovable Grains case.

Lovable Grains' products came in recyclable, compostable cardboard canisters with plastic tops. One day, CEO Susan Jones's production head, Rafer Williams, entered her office with a question.

"Susan, we're excited about the new package design. But, would you like to continue to use the same brown plastic tops? We have such a large quantity that we'll be set for at least half the year."

"Rafer, if the cost savings are obvious, why are you asking me this question?" Susan replied.

"Well," Rafer answered, "the existing tops are the only part of our packaging that is not recyclable. A recyclable top would be twice the price. You've talked about how important recyclable packaging is to our brand. What should I do? I guess we could make the change when we've run out."

Susan thought for a moment: "No, Rafer, buy new, recyclable covers now."

This is a clear example of a leader "walking the talk." Raising and then immediately dealing with troublesome issues are important in transformational leadership. Team members care more what you do, or don't do, than what you say. Susan's staff will respect her for making the right decision, Lovable Grains' customers will undoubtedly appreciate the change, and the company's image will benefit.

Caring about individual team members and relating warmly and intensely to them

As you will immediately recognize, this final transformational leadership skill is a natural part of The Universal Management Principle: *"People don't care how much you know until they know how much you care."* If team members don't feel you care about them, they are not going to get behind your plan. You get what you give.

As mentioned above, the 3x3x3 meetings are an excellent forum for spending one-on-one time with each team member. Periodic team celebrations when key benchmarks are achieved also evidence your commitment.

63

If you are excited about transformational leadership, you may now have two additional questions: "What's the proof that transformational leadership *really works*?" and "Can I learn it?"

To answer the first question, a review of transformational leadership research over twenty-five years and 113 studies concludes: "Overall, our results support that transformational leaders lead not only their individual followers but also their teams and organizations to achieve higher levels of performance."[21]

What is especially interesting is that these studies are not about celebrity CEOs; rather, they cover a broad spectrum of managers. The research shows If you believe you are capable of making a breakthrough, you likely will. More often than not, your vision and game plan will usher in a new era of superior team performance and organizational growth.

Regarding the second question, learning transformational leadership, research shows that it can definitely be taught. An early study, for example, concerned twenty branch bank managers, half of whom received transformational leadership training and half of whom did not.[22] The training consisted of a one-day group seminar about what a transformational leader does followed by four individual coaching sessions.

Five months later, the branches run by managers who had received training saw personal loan sales increased by 39 percent, far exceeding the results of branches where the manager had not been trained.

Let me end this chapter by saying that, in my experience, there are few more enjoyable work experiences than celebrating a game plan victory. You and your team will bask in the pride of collective achievement and the prospect of a better future for all.

21 Gang Wang *et al.*, "Transformational Leadership and Performance Across Criteria and Levels: A Meta-Analytic Review of 25 Years of Research," *Group & Organization Management* 36, no.2 (2011): 223-270.
22 Julian Barling, Tom Weber, and E. Kevin Kelloway, "Effects of Transformational Leadership Training on Attitudinal and Financial Outcomes: A Field Experiment," *Journal of Applied Psychology* 81, no. 6 (1996): 827-832.

Transformational Leadership
Challenge Questions

1. Looking at the next couple years, what is your vision for your team (or your company)? Consider your aspirations, challenges, resources, and team capabilities.

_____

_____

_____

_____

_____

_____

2. What are your strengths that will help you as a transformational leader? What skills do you need to develop?

_____

_____

_____

_____

_____

_____

3. After reviewing the vision game plan section of this chapter, are you prepared to put in the time and effort to develop your game plan and to execute it?

_____

_____

_____

_____

_____

_____

Chapter 8

Power of the Team

Deborah Sandez aspires to be the type of transformational leader described in the last chapter. She heads the medical simulation laboratory (MSL at a large Southern teaching hospital. She and her staff create mannequins and body part models on which doctors can practice surgical skills. Over the last ten years, her team has produced eye-balls for cataract surgery, torsos with bullet wounds, artificial larynxes, sculpted hearts, natural and Caesarean birthing simulators, and many more innovative teaching devices.

Deborah's department is a key research and development arm of the hospital. Its funding level, however, depends primarily on the hospital's surplus. In lean years, Deborah spends as much time raising outside money as she does working in her lab.

Wouldn't it be great, she dreams, if MSL had at least one deep-pocket, multi-year funder? The obvious choice, she knows, would be the military, which already buys some of MSL's products, like its wounded soldier mannequin. With the defense budget increasing, she realizes that her lab has a significant opportunity to meet more of the military's medical training needs.

To explain her vision, Deborah calls a meeting of her senior staff: Tom Speedine (Senior Engineer), Ann Cooper (Design Head), Bob Mullaney (Director of Outside Sales), and Tracy Vaugn (Controller).

"I want us to go after a large, ongoing defense contract," she tells them. "What are your ideas?" Everyone weighs in on the best ways to engage the different service branches. After much animated discussion, she and her team develop an "Op Military Sales" game plan with these assignments:

- Deborah and Bob – Contact each military branch's surgical head to promote a long-term contract.

- Tom and Ann – Interview military doctors to assess training needs and then build prototypes of desired devices.

- Tracy – Prepare volume pricing on existing and new products.

Over the next three months, Deborah and her team plunge ahead, all the while carrying their regular workload. The Marine Corps turns out to be the most interested military branch. Bob has built a strong relationship with Rear Admiral Mary Kramer, the Marines' chief medical officer.

"If your lab can help us train medics, nurses, and doctors in repairing injuries caused by improvised explosive devices – the damage our soldiers are suffering is quite extensive – we're eager to work with you," she has told him. Her surgical staff has met several times with Tom and Ann to discuss the necessary training models.

In the midst of these serious discussions, the hospital's CEO suddenly throws Deborah a curveball. "Deborah," she tells her, "you know I've been supportive so far of your military sales initiative, but we are a teaching hospital. Your goal is admirable, but unless you land a contract in the next month, I'm afraid that you will have to focus all your team's efforts on our current training needs."

Deborah tells her team the nerve-rattling news. "Look, she's given us a month," Bob responds. "We can beat the deadline." Right after the meeting ends, he calls Admiral Kramer. He has been awaiting her decision on a three-year agreement.

"I'm sorry," her assistant tells Bob. "The Admiral will be on vacation until a week from this Thursday, and when she gets back, she has a lot of items on her schedule. I doubt the MSL agreement will be her top priority. I'll have to get back to you when she makes her formal decision."

Bob rushes in to Ann's office, then asks Tom to join them. "Now, I'm the one who needs ideas," he says, explaining the time crisis. "How can we get the Admiral excited about moving forward as soon as she returns from vacation?"

> "
>
> **The greatest leader is not necessarily the one who does the greatest things. He is the one that gets the people to do the greatest things."**
>
> – Ronald Reagan

"Here's a dramatic move," Ann offers. "How about filling her office with our training devices? We can arrange them around our wounded soldier mannequin. We'll put him in a Marine Corps uniform and make the body wounds and the exposed body cavity look like he's just been hit by an IED."

"That will get her attention," Bob responds. "Let me phone back her assistant and see if she'll allow us to do this."

Bob, Ann, and Tom are on pins and needles as Bob makes the second call. The assistant seems excited about the idea but replies that she'll have to get permission from the Admiral's senior staff.

An hour later, as Bob waits tensely at his phone, she calls back: "It's a go."

A smile on his face, Bob calls his colleagues back to his office. "We have permission," he reports. "We can work this weekend to gather and pack all the products. Let's get Tracy involved, too, for a pricing list. I'll brief Deborah that we'll have everything ready by next Tuesday afternoon. Deborah and I can then fly out to Washington on Wednesday to set up the display in the Admiral's office. We'll even stay over in D.C. that night and call her late Thursday morning. If we can get in to see her that afternoon, maybe we can sew up the deal."

The plan goes well. Admiral Kramer is so impressed by the MSL models that she calls Bob's cell even before he has a

chance to call her. She agrees to a late afternoon meeting at which, after a pricing negotiation, she hands Deborah and Bob an initialed agreement.

The next day Deborah, Bob, Tom, Ann, and Tracy meet for a celebratory lunch with "high fives" all around.

This story illustrates that it is *the team* that is ultimately responsible for realizing the transformational leader's vision. Through creative collaboration, mutual support, and combined energy, the team becomes an unstoppable force.

There is strong research evidence that transformational leaders achieve the best results by working through their teams in just this way:

> **... transformational leaders motivate followers by emphasizing the follower's ties to the collective group, fostering team identity and team potency and efficacy.**
> **... transformational leadership generally shows the highest relationship with team performance [versus] individual and organizational performance..."** [23]

23 Gang Wang *et al.*, "Transformational Leadership and Performance Across Criteria and Levels: A Meta-Analytic Review of 25 Years of Research," *Group & Organization Management* 36, no.2 (2011): 223-270.

How can you, as a transformational leader, harness this team power? The first step is to ask yourself, "Is my team ready? In fact, is my team *really a team*?" You may simply be managing a work group whose members are only partially engaged with each other.

> **"What I have learned is that people become motivated when you guide them to the source of their own power and when you make heroes out of employees who personify what you want to see in the organization."**
>
> – Anita Roddick,
> founder of The Body Shop

If so, build trust and closer relationships by bringing team members together – for example, by organizing social or sports events, lunch-and-learns, training activities, or brainstorming sessions. Social interaction develops team member empathy, understanding, liking, and respect.

Each of your team members should feel that his or her sense of professionalism is closely tied to the team's accomplishments and values. Furthermore, team members must like each other well enough to support each other. Enthusiastic cooperation leads to remarkable results.

According to the *Harvard Business Review,*[24] three traits characterize particularly successful teams (the definitions following each term are mine):

1. *Trust* – Team members are willing to be open and vulnerable with each other, truthful and supportive.

2. *Group Identity* – Team members feel that the team's success will fulfill their own needs and aspirations, and that their values are aligned with the team's.

3. *Group Efficacy* – Team members are confident they possess the skills and ability to execute the game plan and realize their leader's visionary goals.

To get this cohesion, you may have to overcome a history of team member conflict, misunderstandings, or rivalries. This friction usually subsides when team members get to know each other better. How many times have you heard an admission like, "Joe really isn't such a bad guy after all. I didn't know his background played such an important part in the way he expresses himself. Actually, he's a likeable guy." Or, "Susan's illness

---

24 Vanessa Urch Druskat and Steven B. Wolff, "Building the Emotional Intelligence of Groups," *Harvard Business Review,* March 2001, https://hbr.org/2001/03/building-the-emotional-intelligence-of-groups

must have been the reason she's been acting the way she has. I understand her now and feel more prepared to work with her."

Of course, not all troubled relationships can be repaired. When strife continues, you, as the team leader, must deal with it constructively. Start by conducting individual meetings to understand each aggrieved team member's viewpoint. Then, bring the parties together for open discussion. Take whatever heat these frank conversations may provoke – maybe you are at fault, too? More often than not, team members will gradually come to understand each other and agree to put aside their differences for the good of the team, especially if you make it clear that this is what must be.

Your serving as a role model is equally important in generating team motivation. Radiate positivity. Be open with your team members to engender their trust and respect. Express pride in them, citing their past achievements and pres-

> ## "
> ### Talent wins games, but teamwork and intelligence win championships."
>
> – Michael Jordan

ent capabilities. Even if there are tough obstacles to face, never doubt that your team can overcome them. Such inspiring leadership is the key to victory.

Remember to reward your team, both, as stated earlier, when benchmarks are achieved and when the game plan succeeds. Not only do your team members deserve it, you want them to be looking forward to future challenges. Review the rewards chapter in this book for ideas, and look for chances to uses the most powerful rewards like personalized recognition.

Two final suggestions: (1) If you experience setbacks – and every team effort has them – improvise, correct course, and *keep moving forward*. Look upon setbacks as expected and as an opportunity to improve, and (2) always keep in mind that harnessing the power of the team stems from The Universal Management Principle. Do whatever it takes to let team members know you care about them. Make them feel like the champions they will show you they are.

Chapter 9

The End and The Beginning

This final chapter begins with a summary of the motivational techniques in this book. If you choose which ones will best fit your individual team members and the situation – and apply them with a caring touch – you will achieve excellent results.

Leadership Technique	Effect on Team Member Motivation
Autonomy	Puts team members in charge of how they do their jobs and elicits their enthusiasm.
Mastery	Builds team members' skills and confidence, enabling them to become more productive.
Goal-Setting	Focuses team members' efforts on desired results.
Rewards	Incentivize team members and create satisfying work experiences.
Job Enrichment	Makes work so much more interesting, involving, and meaningful.
Fairness	Maintains positive team member attitudes and creates a reciprocal commitment to the manager and the organization.
Transformational Leadership	Creates a vision and inspires team members to work together to achieve it.
Power of the Team	Realizes the leader's vision through a united will to succeed.

Refer to this table to create your own comprehensive team member motivation chart. As I previously indicated, you can use the template at the end of this chapter (see next page) or create your own format. Your chart will become your invaluable guide to motivating your team.

Implementing this book's techniques will require commitment and humility. The commitment part is to dedicate yourself to action. Put aside your doubts. As I have stated, at least fifty years of research studies have shown the effectiveness of the Universal Management Principle and the motivational methods derived from it. You will see yourself becoming a stronger, more respected leader and your team producing the results you want.

The humility part is to recognize that it is first the team, *and then you*, who should receive the lion's share of recognition and rewards. The concept of this book is really very simple: if you care about your team and they know it, they will be motivated to respond with their best efforts. *People don't care how much you know until they know how much you care.*

How I will motivate my team members to excel

Team Member	Autonomy	Mastery	Goal-Setting	Rewards	Job Enrichment	Fairness

www.ingramcontent.com/pod-product-compliance
Lightning Source LLC
Chambersburg PA
CBHW051230200326
41519CB00025B/7318